I0494850

A Ghost Walking Through a Dream

A CURIOUS
COLLECTION
OF HAIKU
AND
ILLUSTRATIONS

A Ghost Walking Through a Dream

a curious
collection
of haiku
and
illustrations

Written, illustrated and designed

by William Carey

A Ghost Walking Through a Dream
A Curious Collection of Haiku and Illustrations
All Rights Reserved.
Copyright © 2017 William Carey
v3.0 r1.0

The opinions expressed in this manuscript are solely the opinions of the author and do not represent the opinions or thoughts of the publisher. The author has represented and warranted full ownership and/or legal right to publish all the materials in this book.

This book may not be reproduced, transmitted, or stored in whole or in part by any means, including graphic, electronic, or mechanical without the express written consent of the publisher except in the case of brief quotations embodied in critical articles and reviews.

Outskirts Press, Inc.
http://www.outskirtspress.com

ISBN: 978-1-4787-8557-6

Haiku, Illustrations and Cover Photo © 2017 William Carey. All rights reserved - used with permission.

1. poetry 2. Illustration I. Title.

Outskirts Press and the "OP" logo are trademarks belonging to Outskirts Press, Inc.

PRINTED IN THE UNITED STATES OF AMERICA

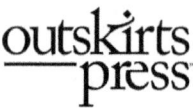

I searched my old haunts

a ghost walking through a dream

a lost memory

— A Haiku by William Carey

Acknowledgements

To my family: my son Mike for your unfailing acknowledgement of my efforts, my daughter Meredith for the editing you did for me; my father, mother and sister Pat for their unconditional support over the years.

To my writers group: Dennis, Eileen, Andy, Margaret, Howard, Roy and Lisa Beth for listening to my work and giving me such valuable feedback. To Phil for giving me the opportunities to read at the poetry nights at the Raue Theater. To Tony and Mike Fleck for your early support.

Table of Contents:

Introduction

scribbling haiku
at two in the morning, words
tossing and turning

The haiku and illustrations in this book were begun nearly 20 years ago. They were created out of a sense of curiosity amusement and spiritual wondering. With the haiku, I could distill complex thoughts and observations down to a seventeen syllable essence in an entertaining way. At first, the illustrations paralleled the haiku as simply doodles or finished drawings on their own. At one point the two disciplines converged as illustrated haiku. So this book represents all of the above: haiku, illustrations and illustrated haiku.

An introduction to a book of haiku would not be complete without an explanation of what a haiku is. A haiku is a 3 line (5-7-5), 17 syllable unrhymed verse. It has been an esteemed form of expression and amusement in Japan since the 16th century. It migrated to the west an has been adopted by many authors and poets including Jack Kerouac, who wrote a whole book of them.

These haiku cover a wide range of subjects: from spiritual to earthy. It has been, for the most part, an intuitive adventure. Although some of the subjects are serious, the purpose is to entertain. So I hope you enjoy this "curious collection of haiku and illustrations".

Enjoy.

Included at the bottom of the pages are the definitions of unusual words
that the author considers critical to the understanding of the verses.
Misunderstanding just one word in such a brief poem can lead to a total
misunderstanding of the entire verse. The author is in no way
underestimating the vocabulary of the reader but words have more
than one definition and sometimes he is using a less familiar one.
Better to err on the side of caution.

In addition to the illustrated haiku, I have included many drawings and
paintings that I have done over the years. I am an incurable doodler, mak-
ing sketches of people and from my imagination. Theses have been placed
throughout the book as accents to the haiku.

Everyday Haiku

knock-kneed day bumping
into itself sighs, smiles and
becomes tomorrow

a dog barks, speaking
in animal tongues, head cocks
knowingly, I bark

lukewarm breeze buffets
my concentration, mocking
short attention span

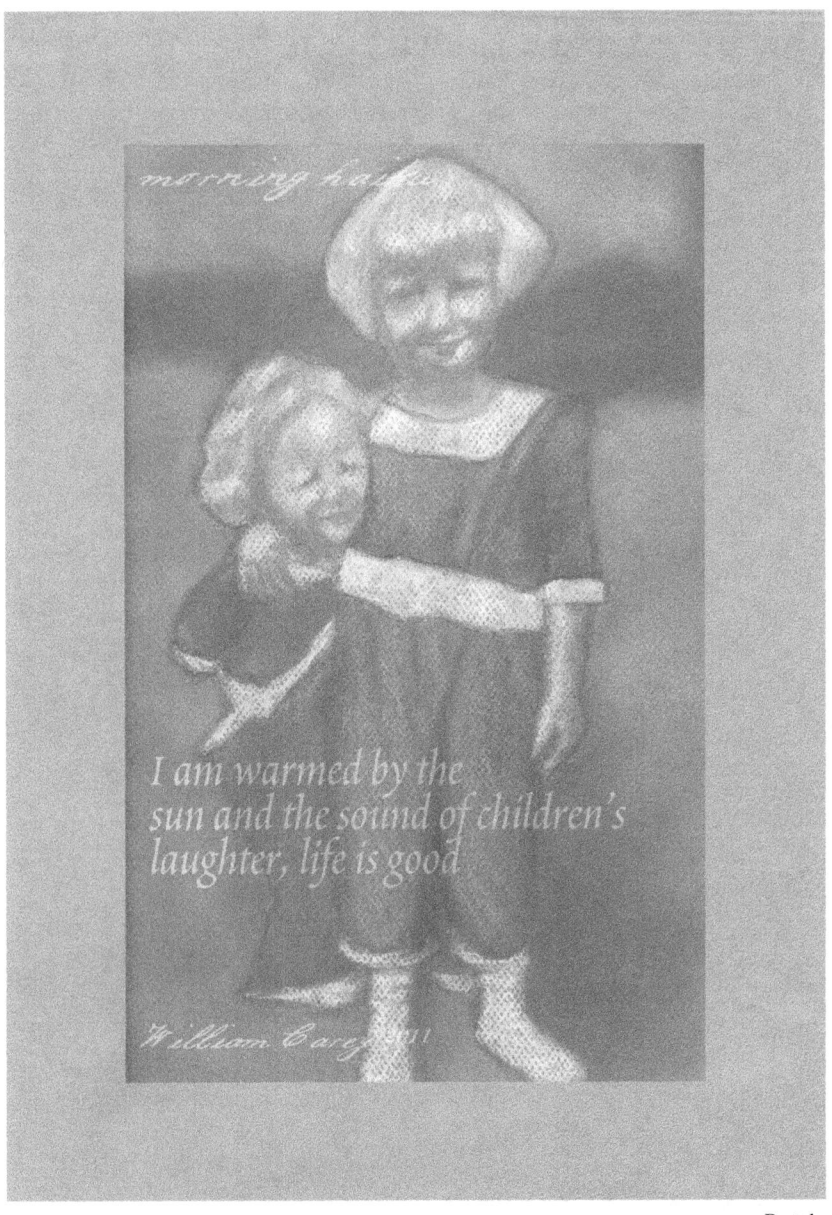

morning ha...

I am warmed by the
sun and the sound of children's
laughter, life is good

William Care...

Pastel

Mundane happenings stumbled upon by a wandering mind.

Spiritual haiku

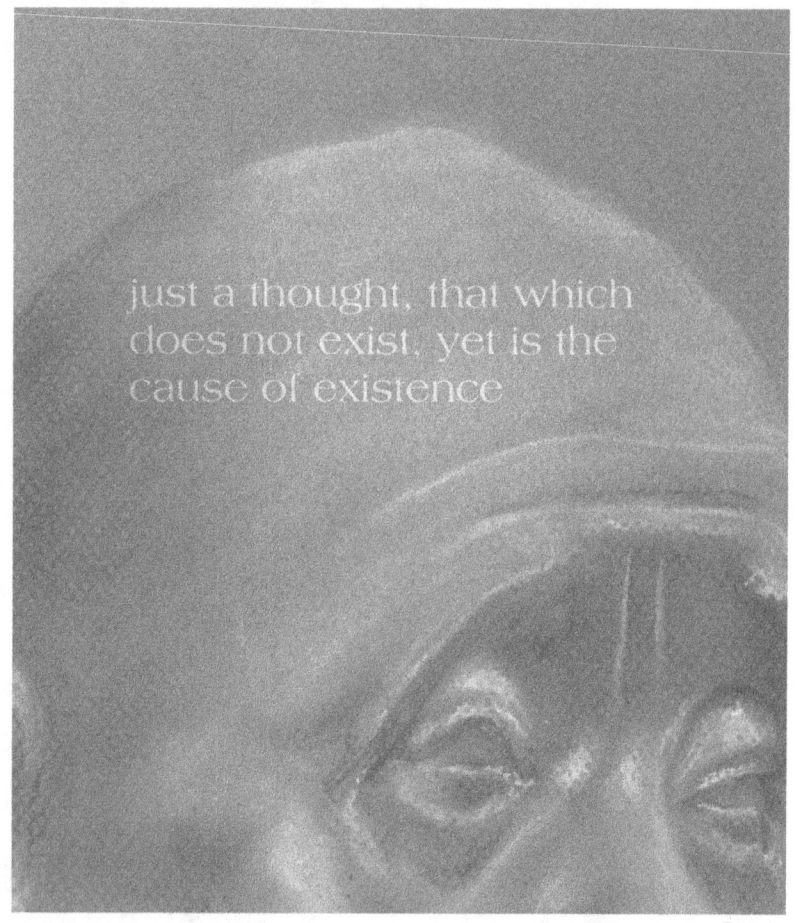

just a thought, that which
does not exist, yet is the
cause of existence

Pastel

a yawn, a wisp of

clarity...sparkling thoughts

resolve into light

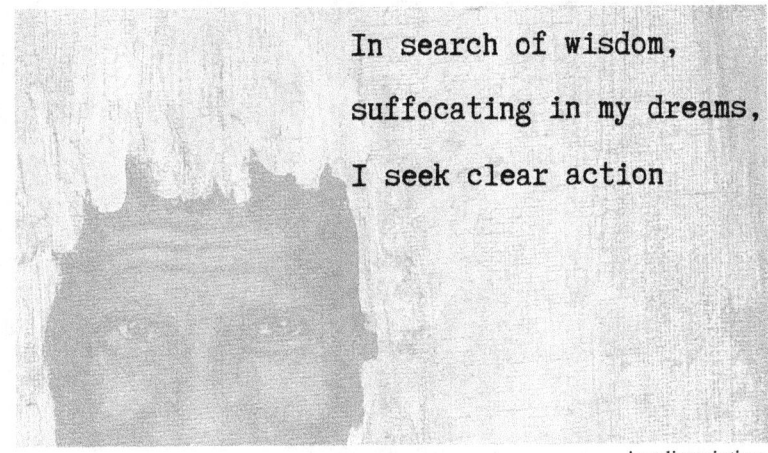

In search of wisdom,

suffocating in my dreams,

I seek clear action

Acrylic painting

breathe deeply, exhale,

we are swept away by winds

we have created

Searching for enlightenment and touching wisdom on the run.

Grim Haiku

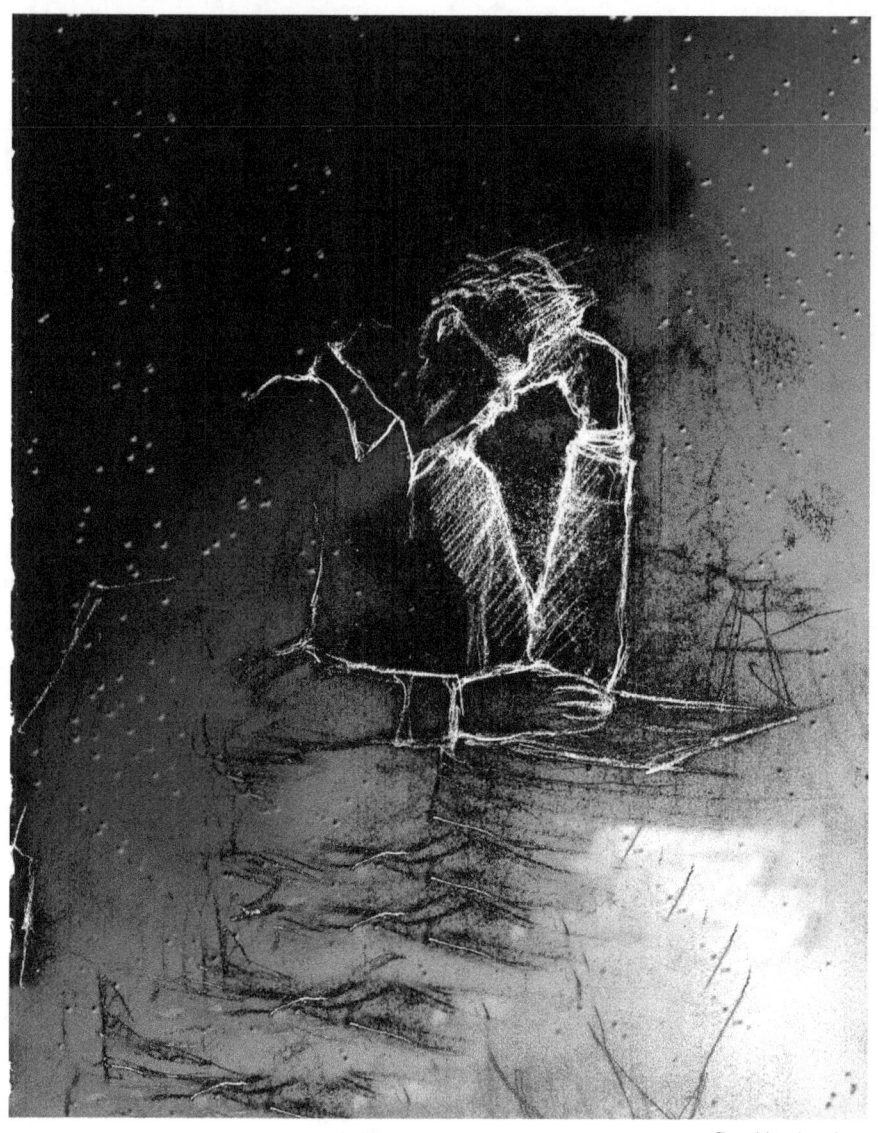

Graphite drawing

wringing a drop of
worth out of a tough day, I
work therefore I am

staring out of the
windows of coffeehouses,
sadly...looking for work

Graphite drawing

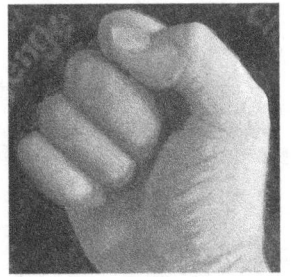

fist of fear clenched with-
in the small of my back, takes
me down from behind

Acrylic

relentless regret
for things done and left undone
don't tell anyone

When you have hit bottom and fallen through.

Romantic and generally Addled Haiku

insouciant love

runs across my path, grinning

unavoidable

you kiss my fingers,

smiling inward (mesmerized,

I am charmed and lost)

my love for you spills

out into my life making

a delightful mess

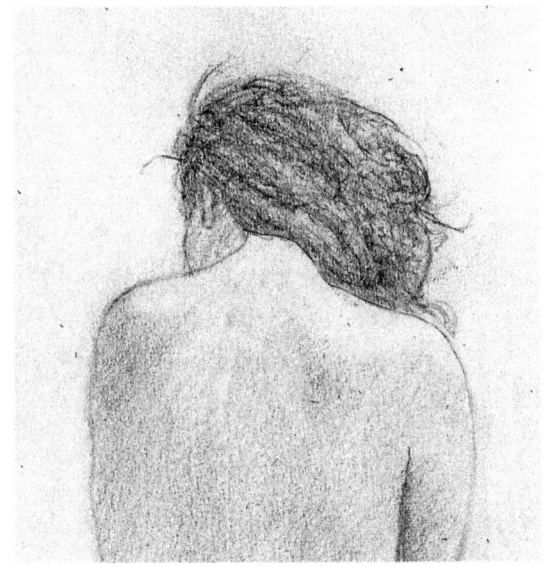

Graphite drawing

love wells up like tears

in my eyes, warm and cleansing

smiling I miss you

Memories of romance seem so surreal and humorous.

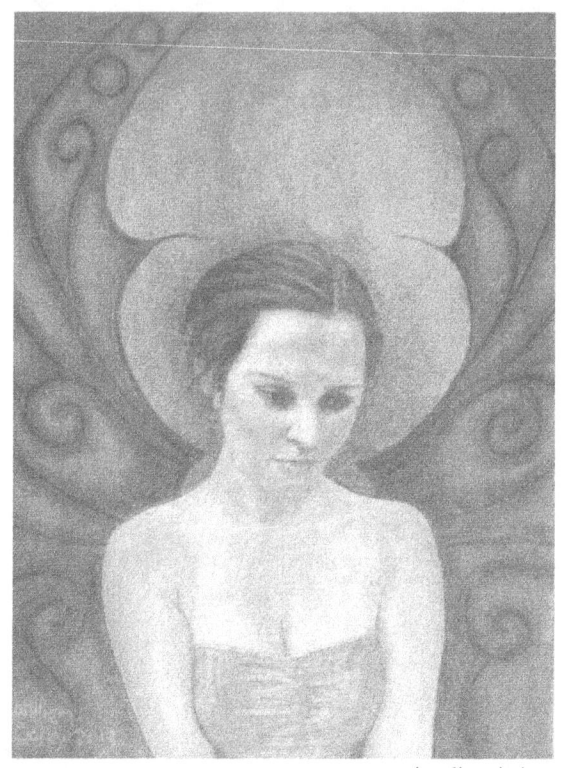

Acrylic painting

unrequited love,

truly...chasing a woman

who wants to be chaste

---

oar leaves the water
eddies blur serenity
insights whirl away

red tail lights flash by
sun sets, the end is here, my
wishes crossed the road

winter turns its cold
shoulder to spring, lighthearted
flowers wave goodbye

Filmy shadows of disappointment under fairy wings.

---

eddy: a circular movement of air or water

low childish whisper

secret carried on hot breath

don't tell anyone

Graphite drawing

cob webs brushed at in

her hair, lingering self doubts

stick to her fingers

sliding out of an

existential chair, smudging

his dissatisfaction

---

existential: refering to a philosophy that emphasizes the isolation of the individual in a hostile universe

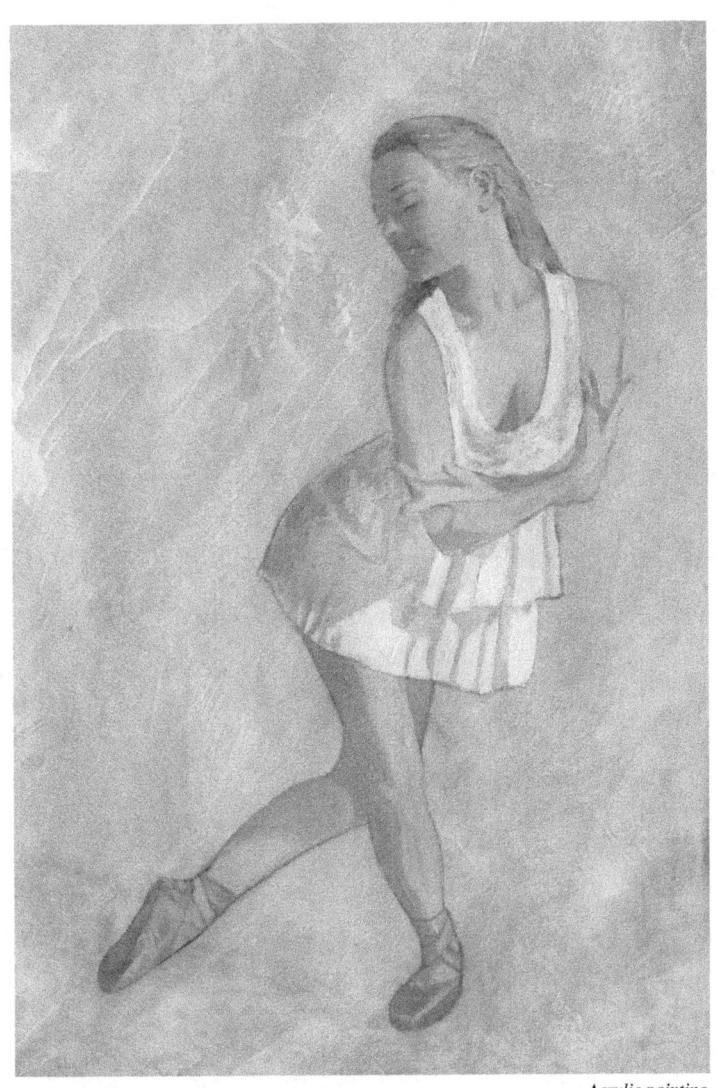

Acrylic painting

```
ballerina braves

the travails of expression

embracing her soul
```

Sometimes life turns its back on you.

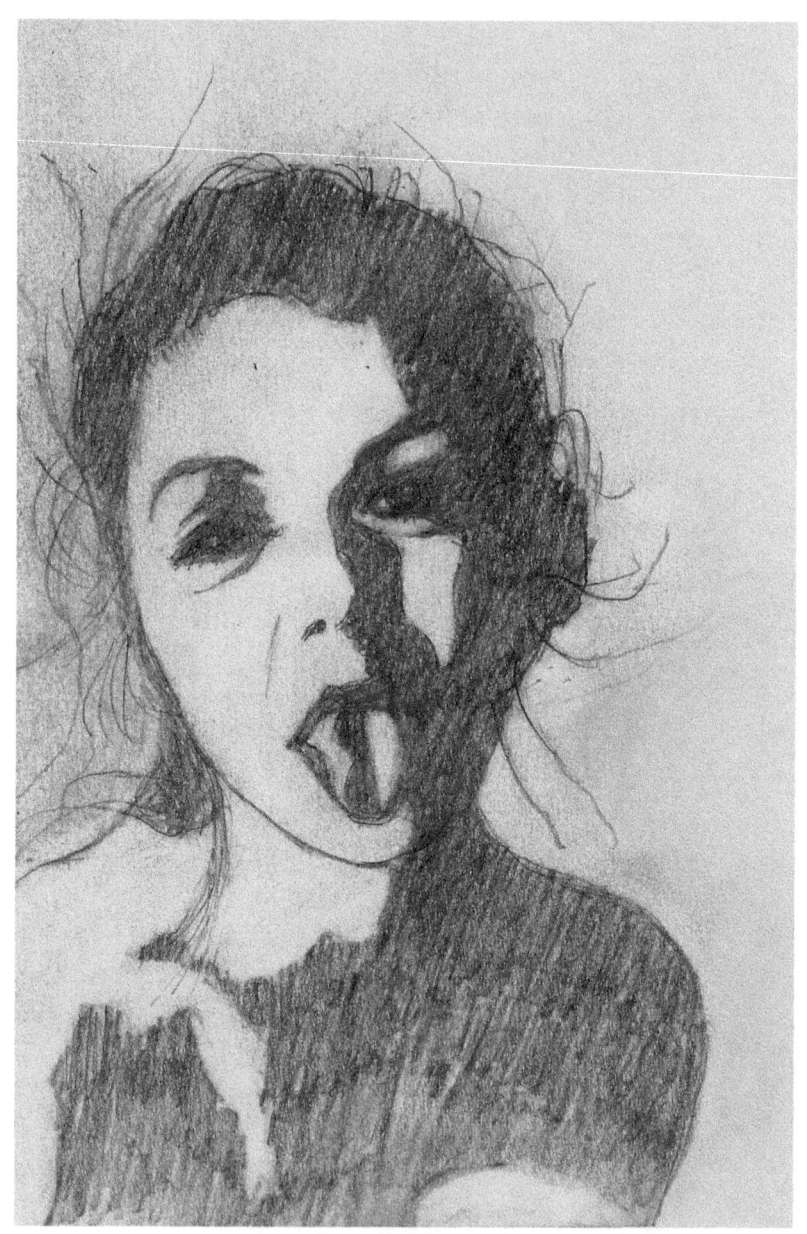

Graphite drawing- *Insouciant Medusa*

Without warning, a cheeky faux pas will stick its tongue out at you.

Faux Pas -an embarrassing or tactless act or remark in a social situation

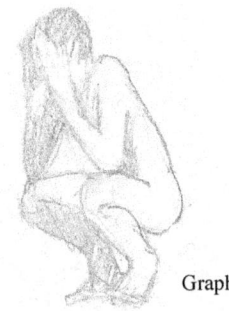

Graphite drawing

torn apart by tough

choices, free will whispers sweet

nothings in my ear

searching for flashes

of inspiration— chasing

lightning in the fog

enduring silence

jarred by laughter, looks

around, yawning and smiling

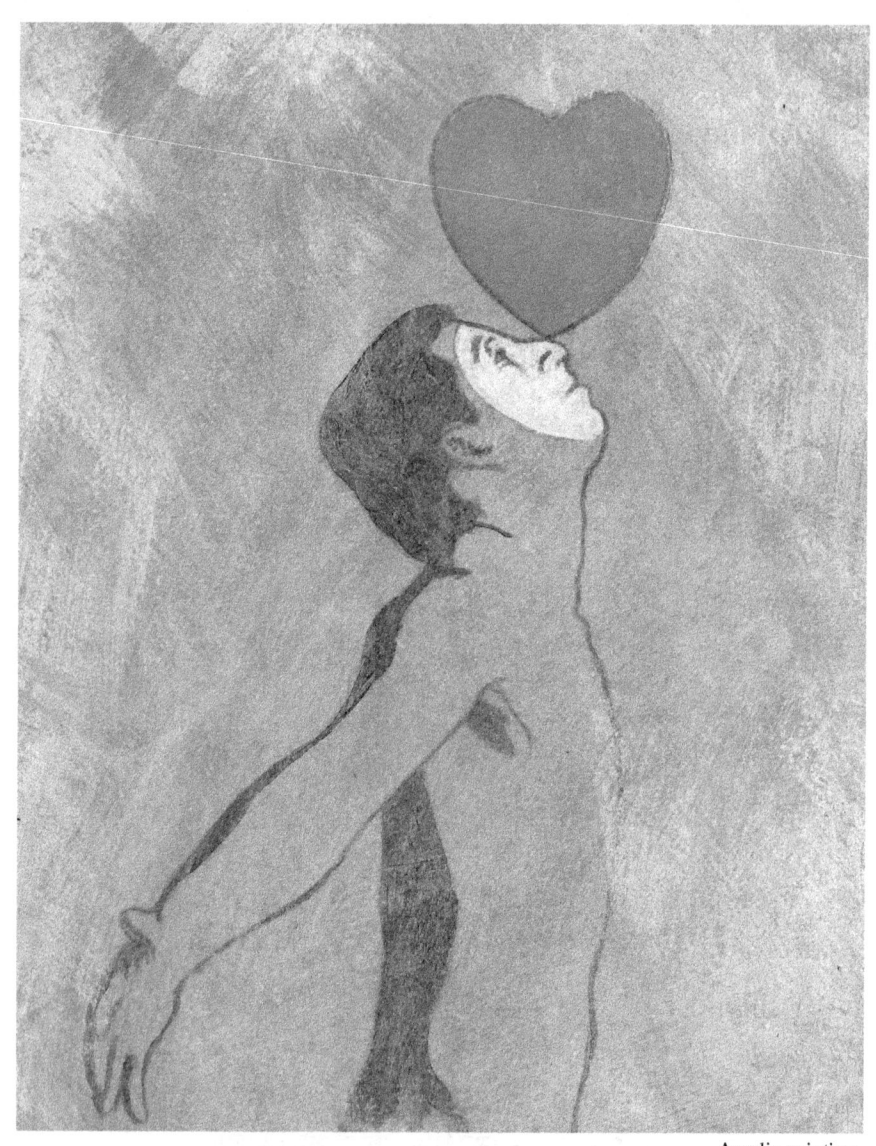

Acrylic painting

a mime in a pose
with a heart on his nose
shows off his love with no clothes

gray dog named ennui

sleeping on his side, stretches

and huffs—what a day

autumn wind hurling

frayed clouds at the horizon

the smell of winter

scribbling haiku

at two in the morning, words

tossing and turning

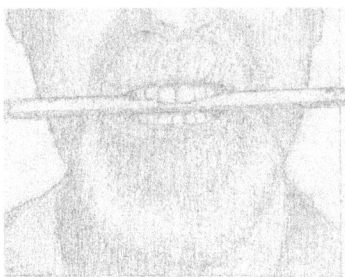

Graphite drawing

Three haiku and a three line poem that rhymes.

---

ennui: a lack of enthusiasm or interest
feral: having escaped from domestication and become wild

broken blister in

the center of my palm,

weekend stigmata

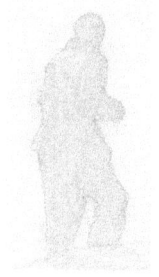

wandering the street

searching for reality

lost soul confers alone

Graphite drawing

ten years staggering

in circles, bumping into

my own creations

---

stigmata: marks or sores corresponding to and resembling the crucifixion wounds of Jesus, some times occurring during religious ecstasy or hysteria

mercurial haiku

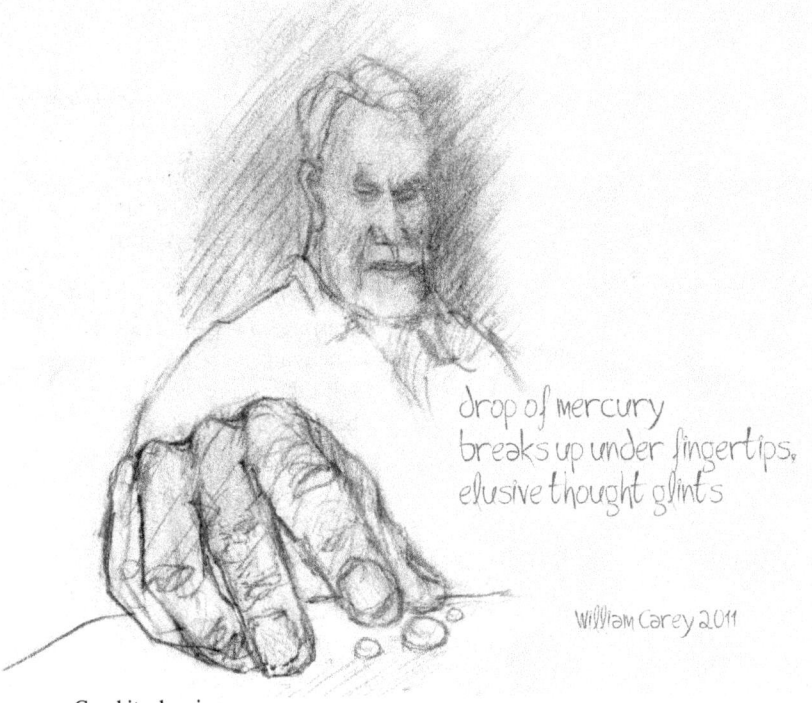

drop of mercury
breaks up under fingertips,
elusive thought glints

William Carey 2011

Graphite drawing

Time slips through my fingers like drops of mercury.

Post-it Show

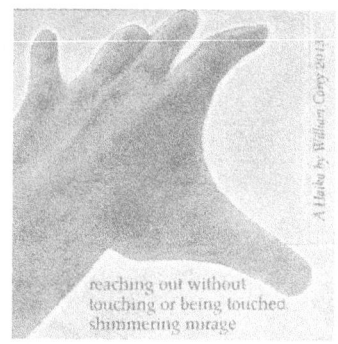

reaching out without
touching or being touched
shimmering mirage

A Haiku by William Carey 2013

Graphite drawing

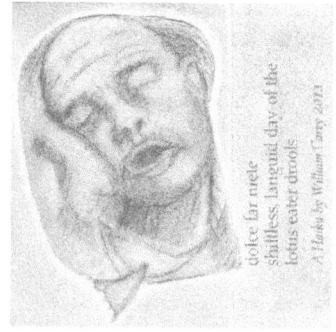

dolce far niete
shiftless, languid day of the
lotus eater drools

A Haiku by William Carey 2011

Graphite drawing

There was an art bar show at the Two Brothers Restaurant in Aurora, IL.

The theme of the show was art on post-it notes. The walls were covered with them. Featured here are a three of my submissions.

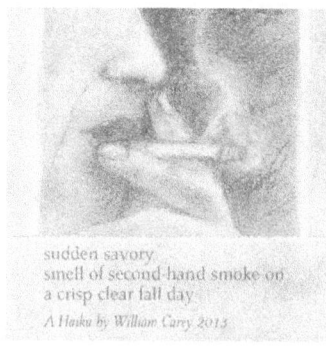

sudden savory
smell of second-hand smoke on
a crisp clear fall day

A Haiku by William Carey 2013

Graphite drawing

---

dolce far niete: doing sweet nothing, blissful laziness

A flock of Haiku

a falcon landed
in my backyard, he found it
unremarkable

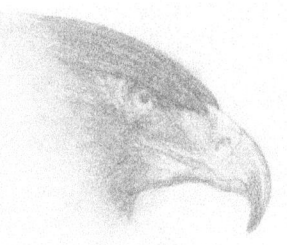

Graphite drawing

a single bird chirps
awakening the dawn of
spring, I close my eyes

a blue birdless sky
silent and empty, searching
for the evening star

hidden bird, lurking
in the black shadows of a
sunny day, chortles

Birds speak to us without uttering a word.

Random Haiku

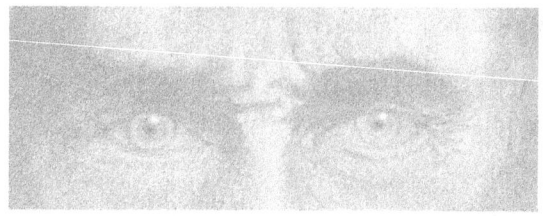

Charcoal drawing

nightmares gobbled up

all my happy dreams last night

bad dreams burp at me

shards of glass on a

cold marble floor, broken dreams

beneath my bare feet

a wilted flower

not yet lifeless, still breathes with

softly fading charm

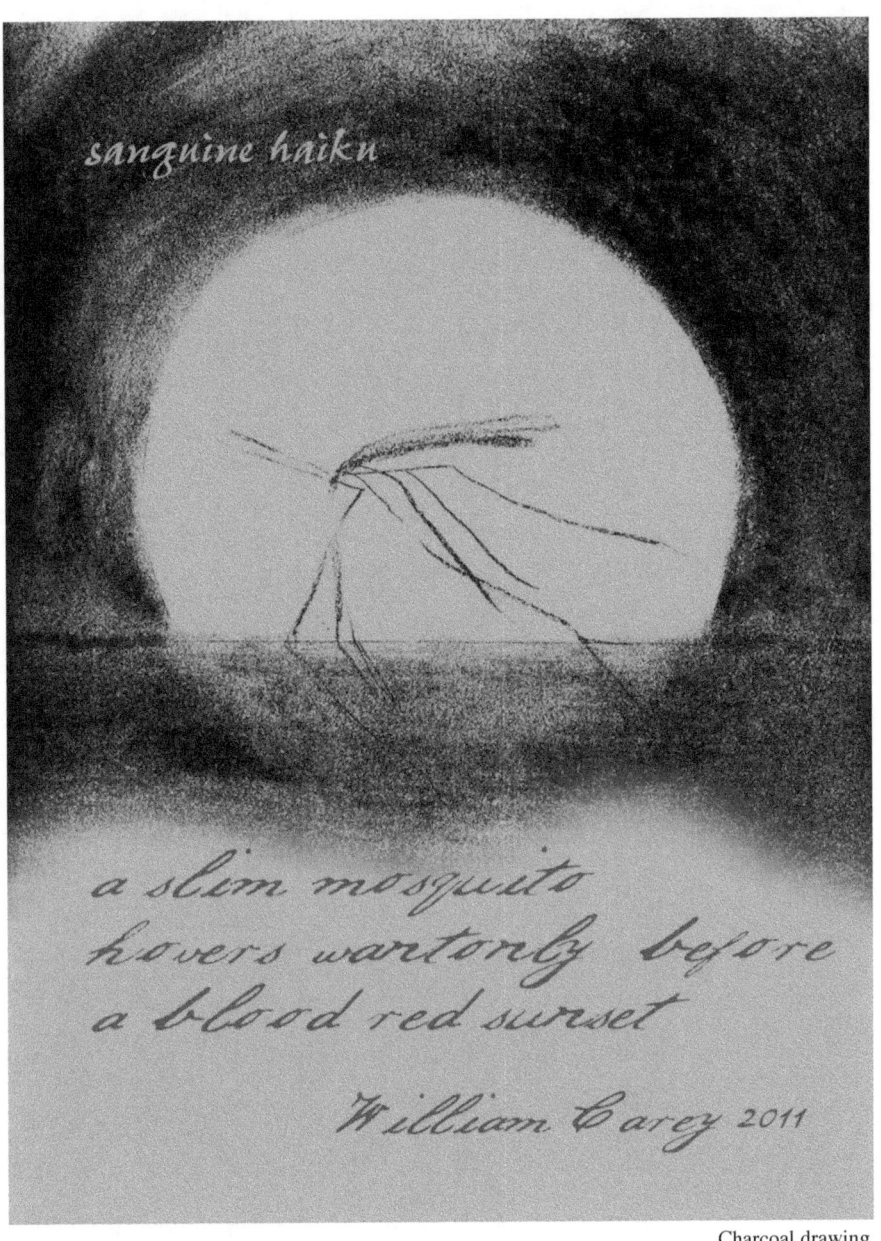

sanguine haiku

a slim mosquito
hovers wantonly before
a blood red sunset

William Carey 2011

Charcoal drawing

Nightmares and bloody insects.

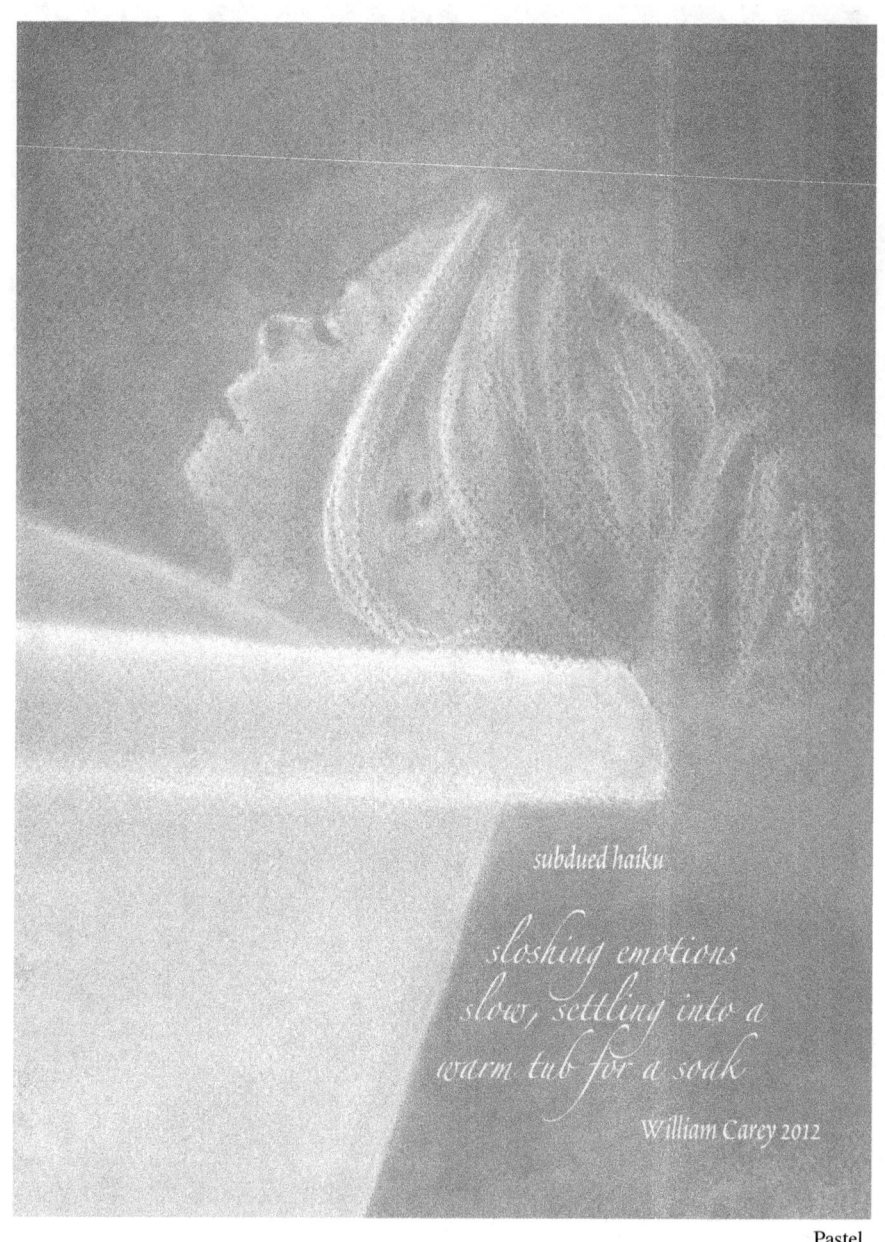

subdued haiku

sloshing emotions
slow, settling into a
warm tub for a soak

William Carey 2012

Pastel

Meditation and relaxation reveal the undulating rhythms of consciousness.

my disembodied

mantra behind calm, closed eyes

overwhelmed by thoughts

closed dappled eyelids

flutter at the warm sunrise,

whispering a dream

raindrops purring on

the roof, gently massage

my insomnia

---

dappled: marked with many spots of color or light
mantra: a sound, word, or phrase that is repeated by someone who is meditating

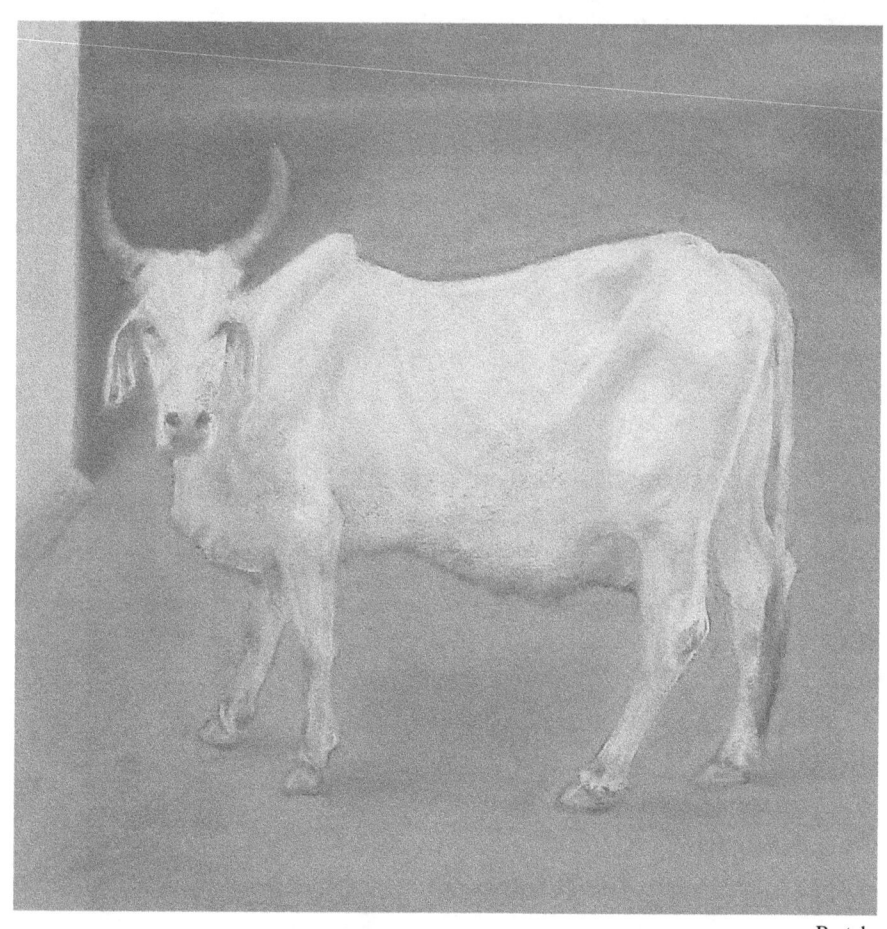

Pastel

```
the universe looks

at me sideways through the eyes

of a sacred cow
```

The mundane and spiritual intermingle effortlessly to create realities.

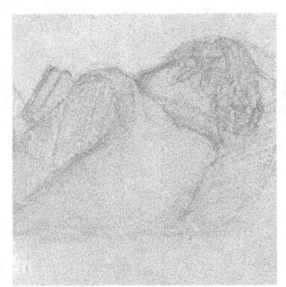

curled up around

Graphite drawing

the tiny print in her bible—

her back to the world

cupcake for breakfast

with purring cats living the

American dream

the fresh pulpy smell

of newsprint, the Sunday Times

heavy in my hands

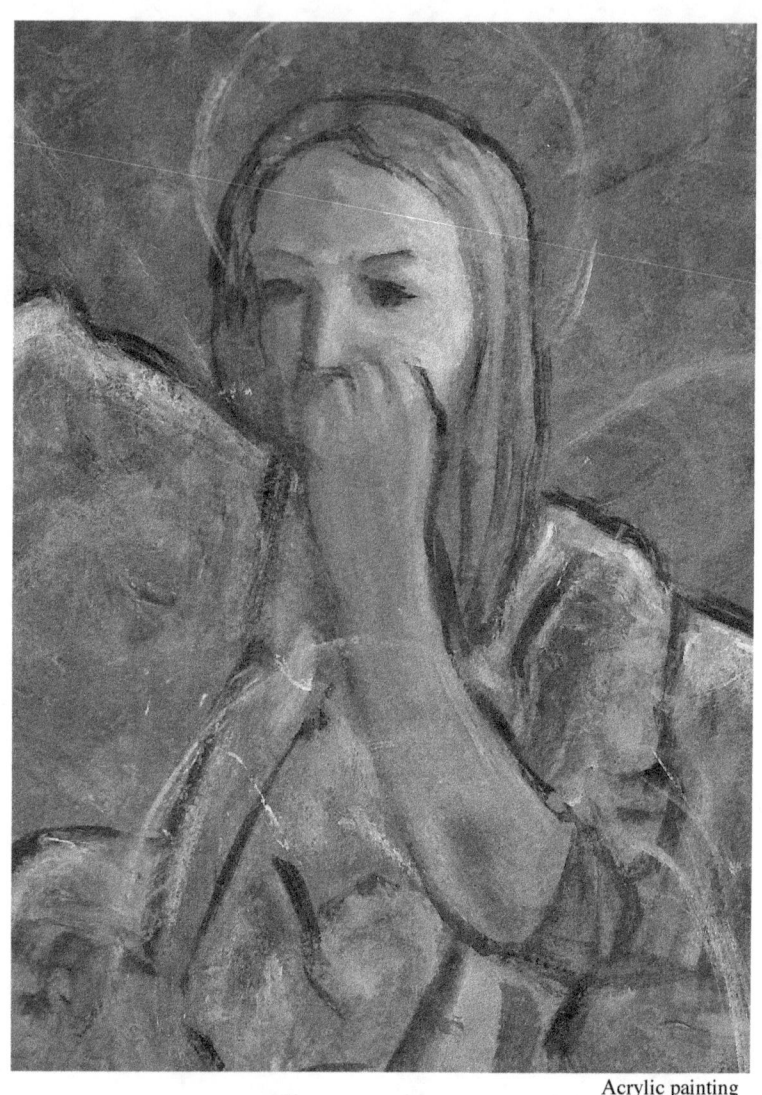

Acrylic painting

pacing back and forth

in her mind on well worn thoughts

and frayed conclusions

back sliding against

the wall, peeking around the

corner at my life

a feral thinker

an emotional gypsy

lone butter fly wings

freehand hearts scrawled in

the hot breath fogging windows

noses pressed to glass

Angst and longing exposed.

Sacred and Profane Haiku

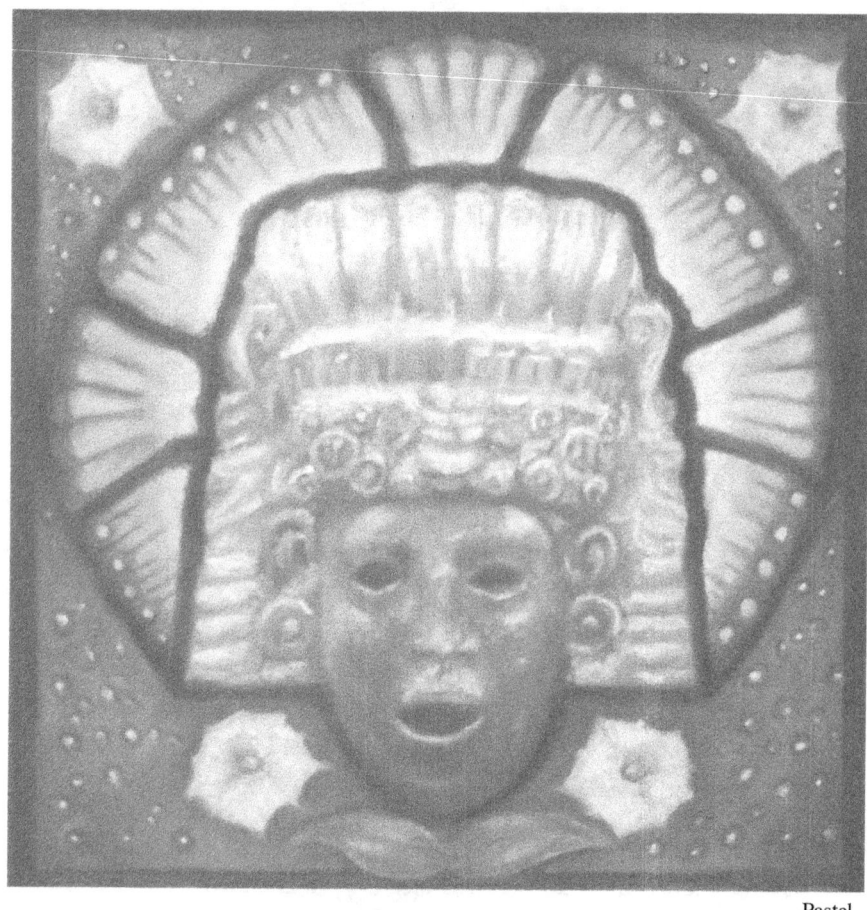

Pastel

God created man,

and then man created gods: a

florescence of gods

Irreverent religious considerations

florescence: a state or period of flourishing

we are windows through

which God enjoys existence

for God's sake enjoy

building an altar

to new God he created,

heretic no more

thank you for all the

good things we have created

here today, amen

-a haiku prayer

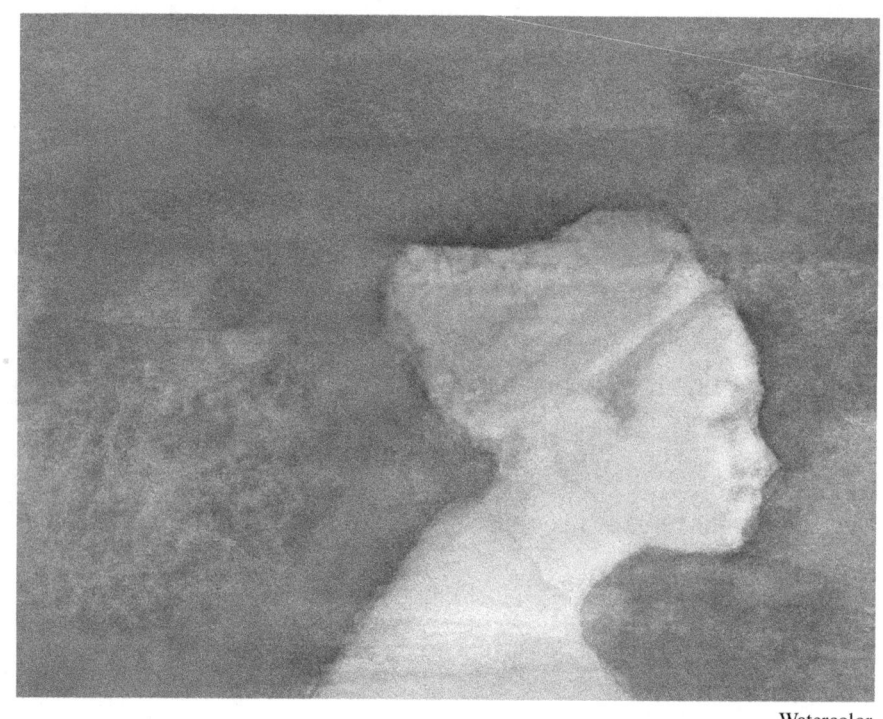

Watercolor

the pilot light of

love sputters in the harsh winds

of vengeful anger

Love, regret and a paradox: transformed emotions.

long rivulets of rain

once a dripping prison ... now

a sanctuary

invisible man

looking at himself in the

mirror, makes a face

shrugging off a dark

cloak heavy with regret, the

sun rises again

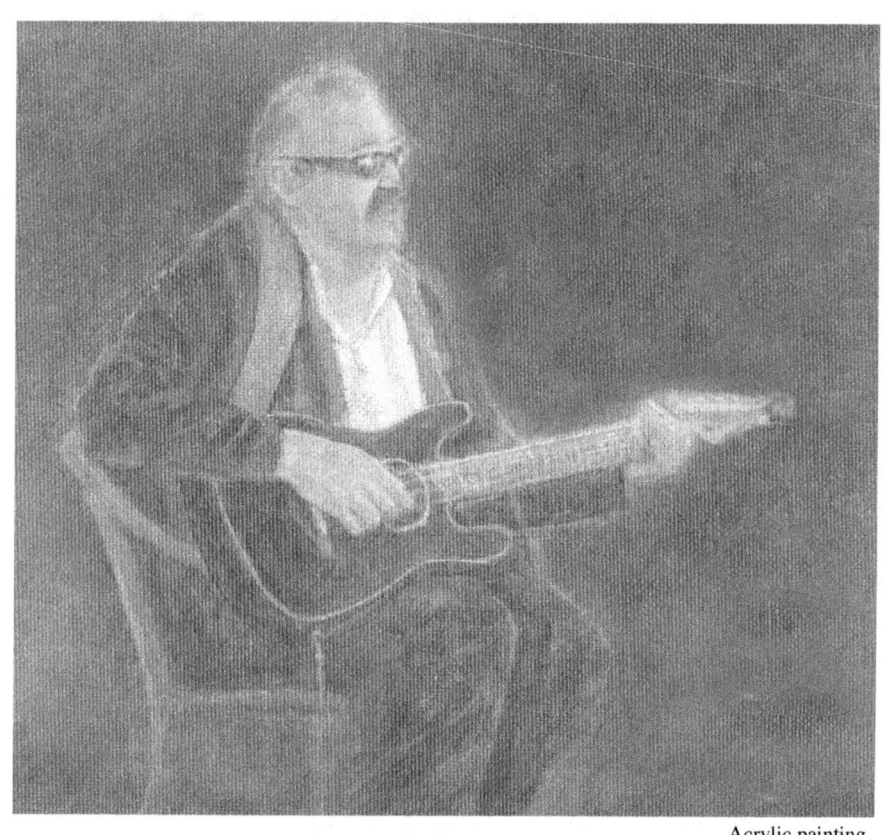

Acrylic painting

musician plays

the blues outside the pearly

gates, passersby smile

---

making angry waves

in a sarcastic sea, caught

in the undertow

dark moments make it

hard to sleep in the darkness

now my soul itches

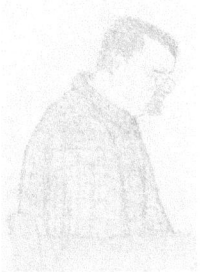

Graphite drawing

eccentric fixture

life percolates around him

sitting at Starbucks

Irreverence , sarcasm, and whimsy comingle.

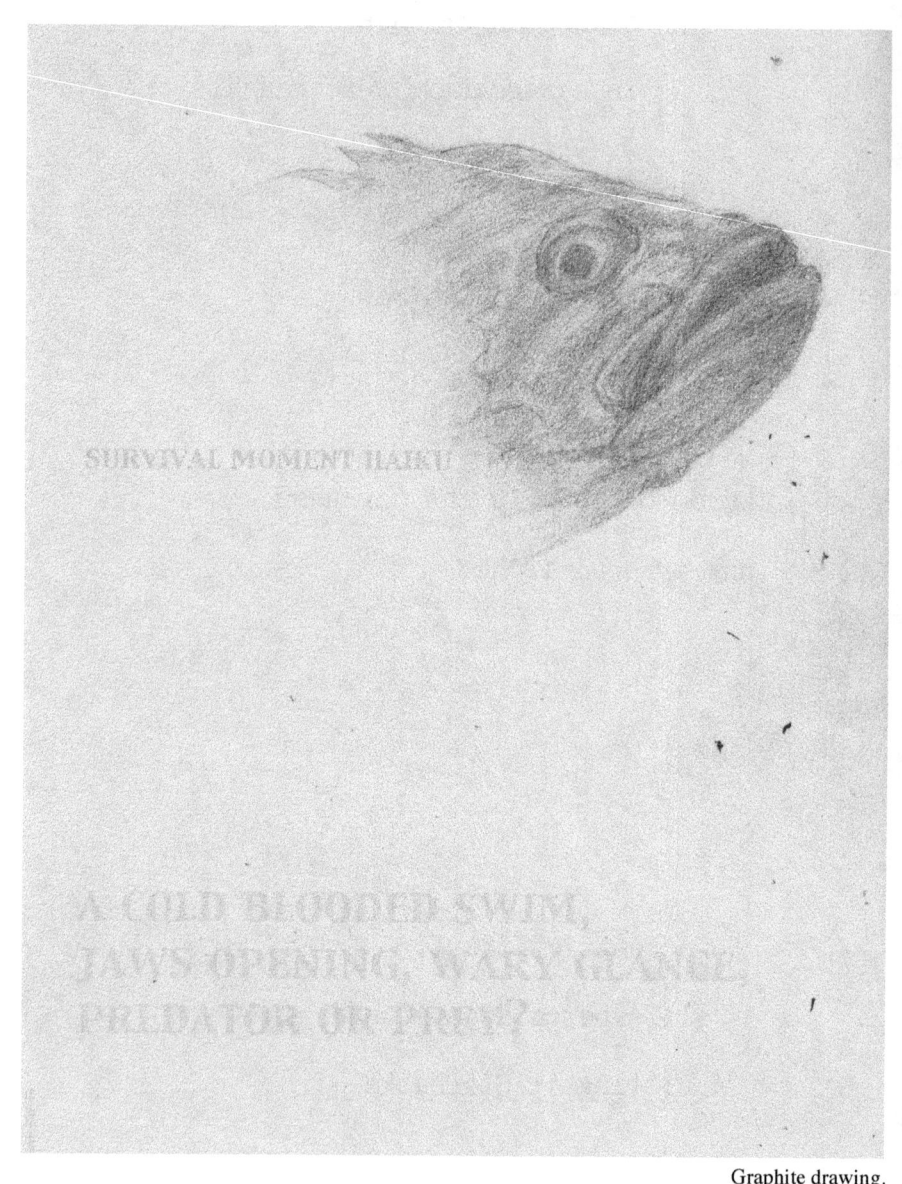

SURVIVAL MOMENT HAIKU

A COLD BLOODED SWIM,
JAWS OPENING, WARY GLANCE,
PREDATOR OR PREY?

Graphite drawing.

Fish swim, birds fly, thoughts never end.

annoyed by aimless

snow flakes without purpose—

dreary cough wheezes

lazy, aimless day,

vague destinations appear

in rearview mirror

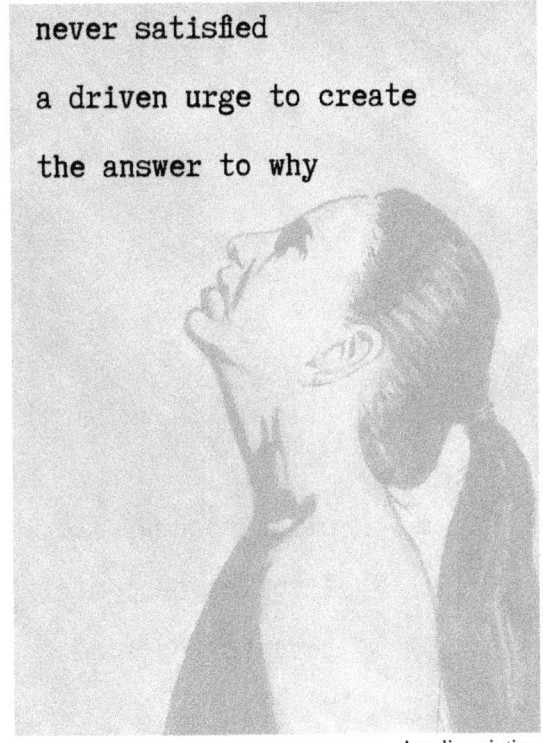

never satisfied

a driven urge to create

the answer to why

Acrylic painting

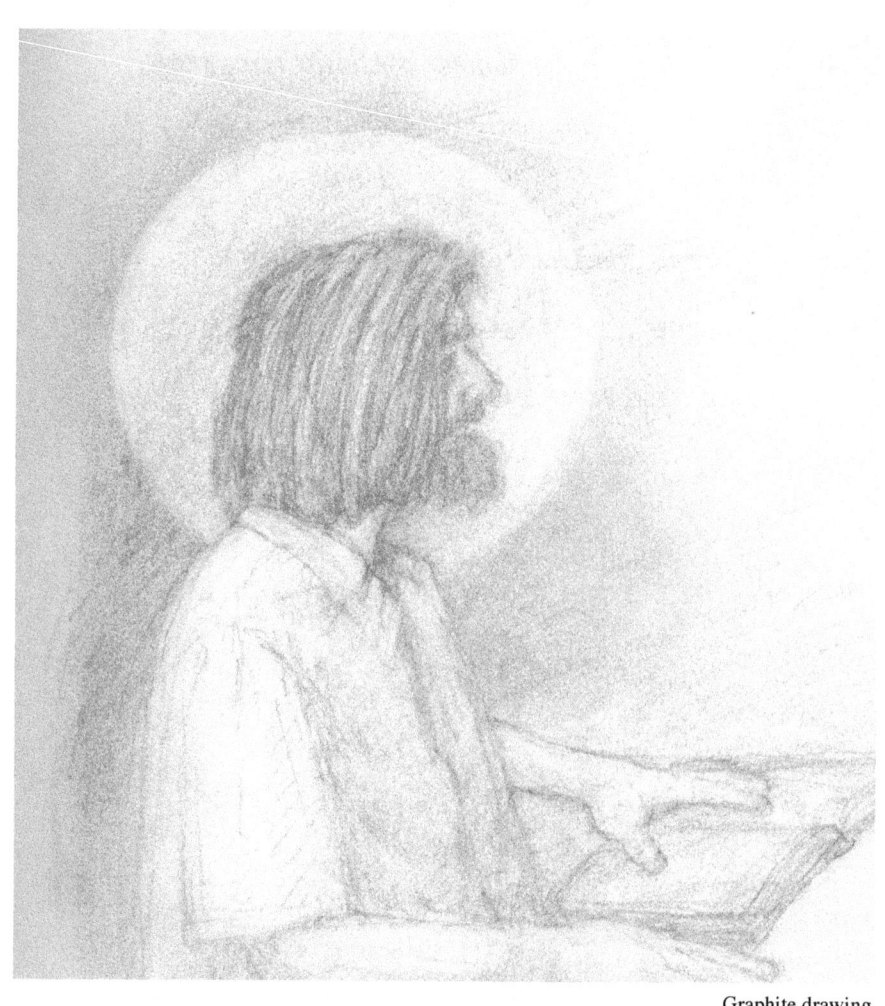

Graphite drawing

plain spoken offering,

a coffee shop minister

reveals the word

Ministers and priests reveal and contrast existential considerations.

a collar-less priest

in public carefully looks

straight ahead, studied

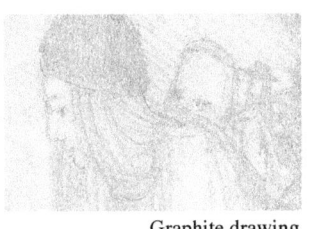

Graphite drawing

starkly aware of

my separateness, observing

others self-absorbed

once ardent search, now

flaccid underlying quest ~

vestigial rudder

---

vestigial: the last small part that remains of something that existed before

window shades are drawn

bright sunlight highlights the dust

the past revealed

enlightenment smiles

from the void, ephemeral,

slowly dissolving

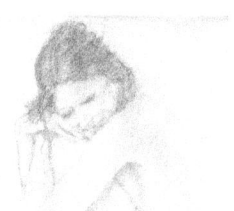

Graphite drawing

oh, Mnemosyne,

the goddess of memory,

please remember me

Enlightenment and distractions collect on the page.

ephemeral: lasting a very short time

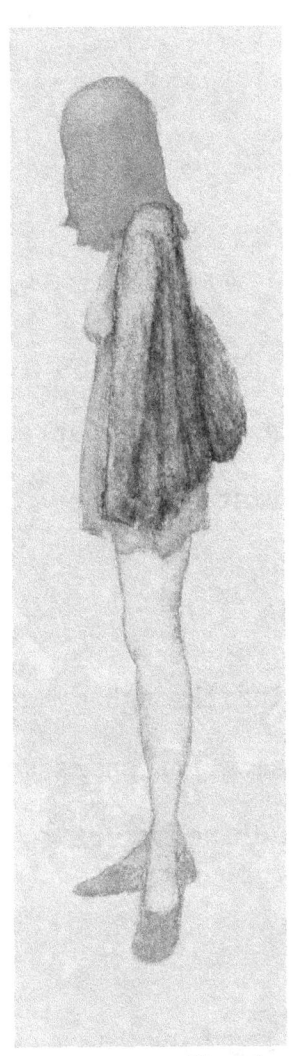

Watercolor

distracted farewell,

she leaves...now a memory

a simplified form

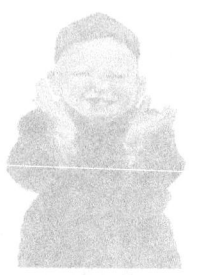

Graphite drawing

as the years go by,

ghosts of the departed fade

at Christmas dinner

drifting through my day

searching for spare words with which

to describe my drift

circling back to

undo the damage done to

others...who have moved on

Memories and regrets cling and fade.

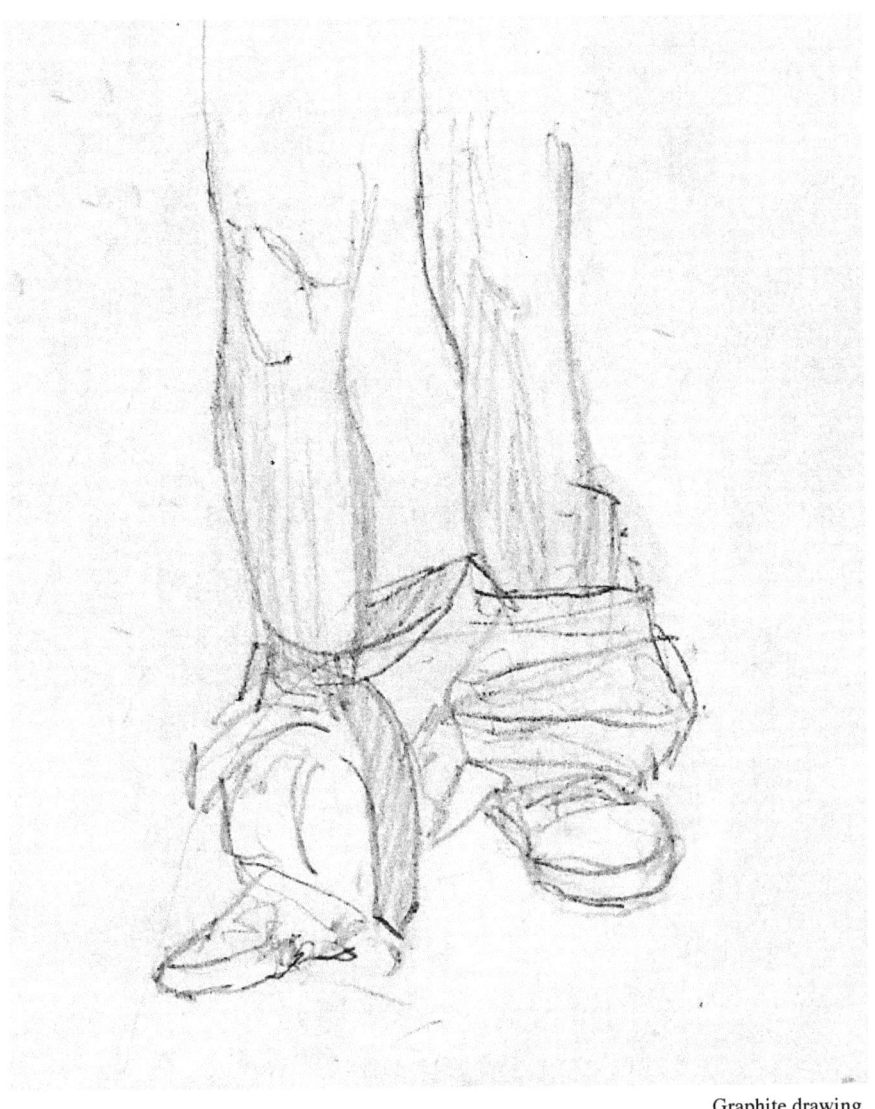

Graphite drawing

hobbled by the truth-

chasing his dreams with his pants

around his ankles

winter is so cold,

lone snowflake falls, touching my

cheek...now a warm tear

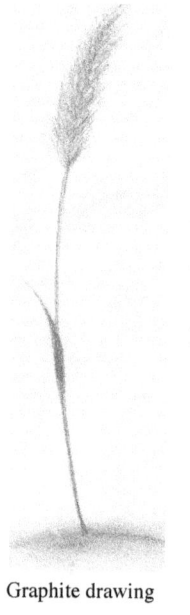

fuzzy plant flitters

wearing frivolous head dress

flailed by a breeze

Graphite drawing

rush in from the cold

fluttering fabric chills legs

chased by winter winds

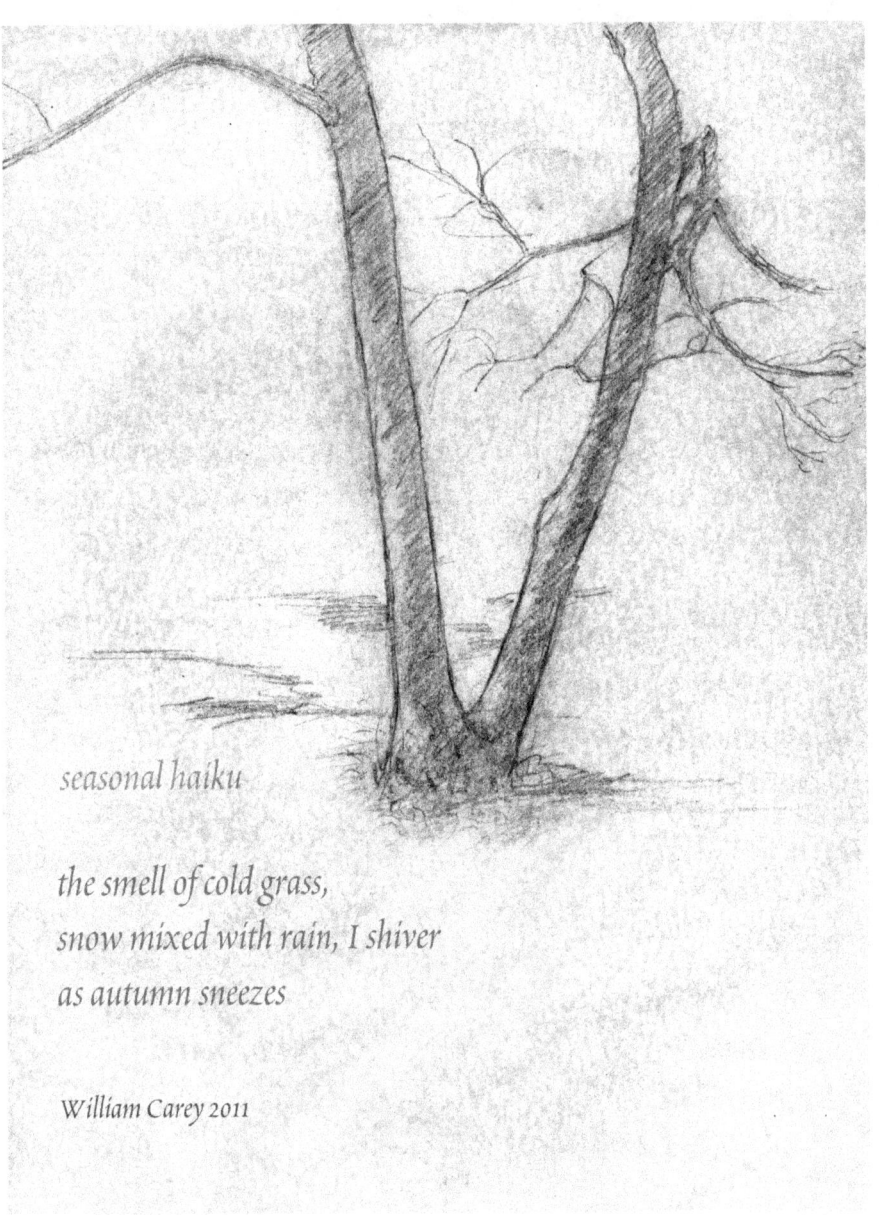

seasonal haiku

the smell of cold grass,
snow mixed with rain, I shiver
as autumn sneezes

William Carey 2011

Graphite drawing

The mood of the seasons affect our senses and emotions.

Dark Subjects

A series of haiku illustrations with black backgrounds and darker subjects. This started out as a series of mime pictures and evolved into a random thoughts on a variety of themes.

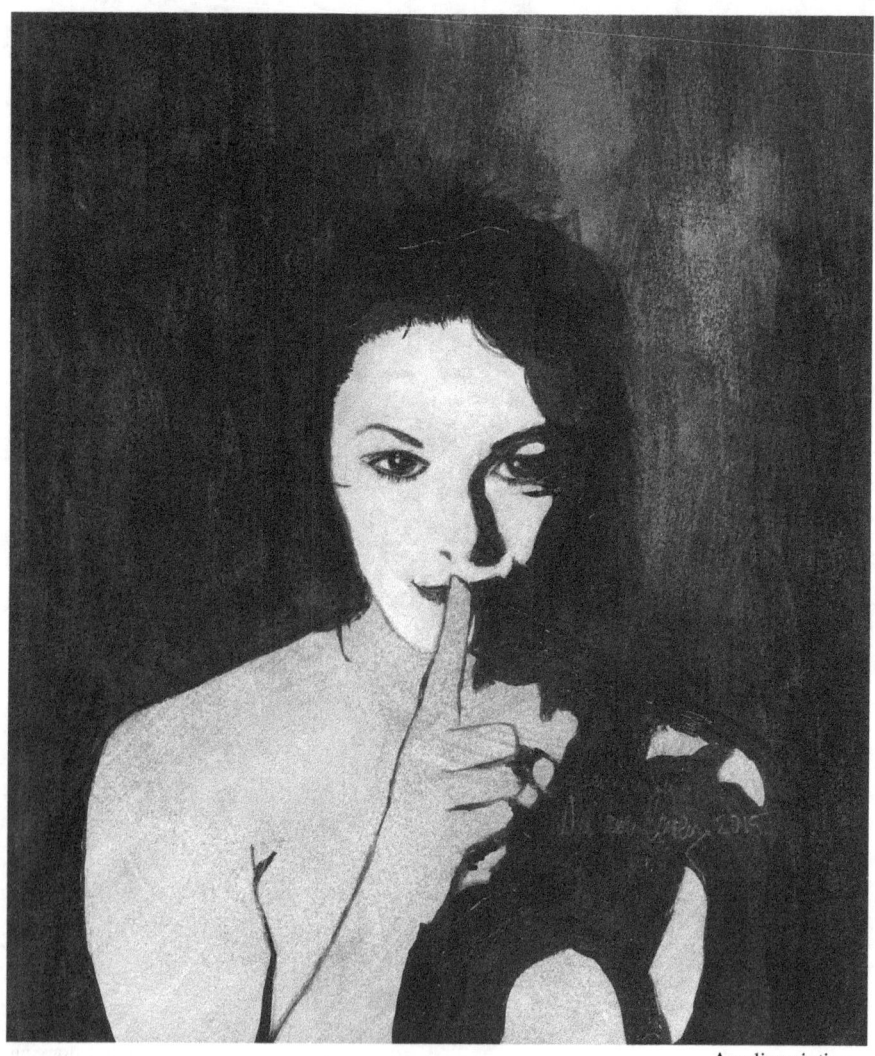

Acrylic painting

```
mime admonishes
the cacophony of life
droll finger to lips
```

droll: curious in a way that provokes dry amusement

...invisible...still...
death poised over shallow breath
...awaiting stillness...

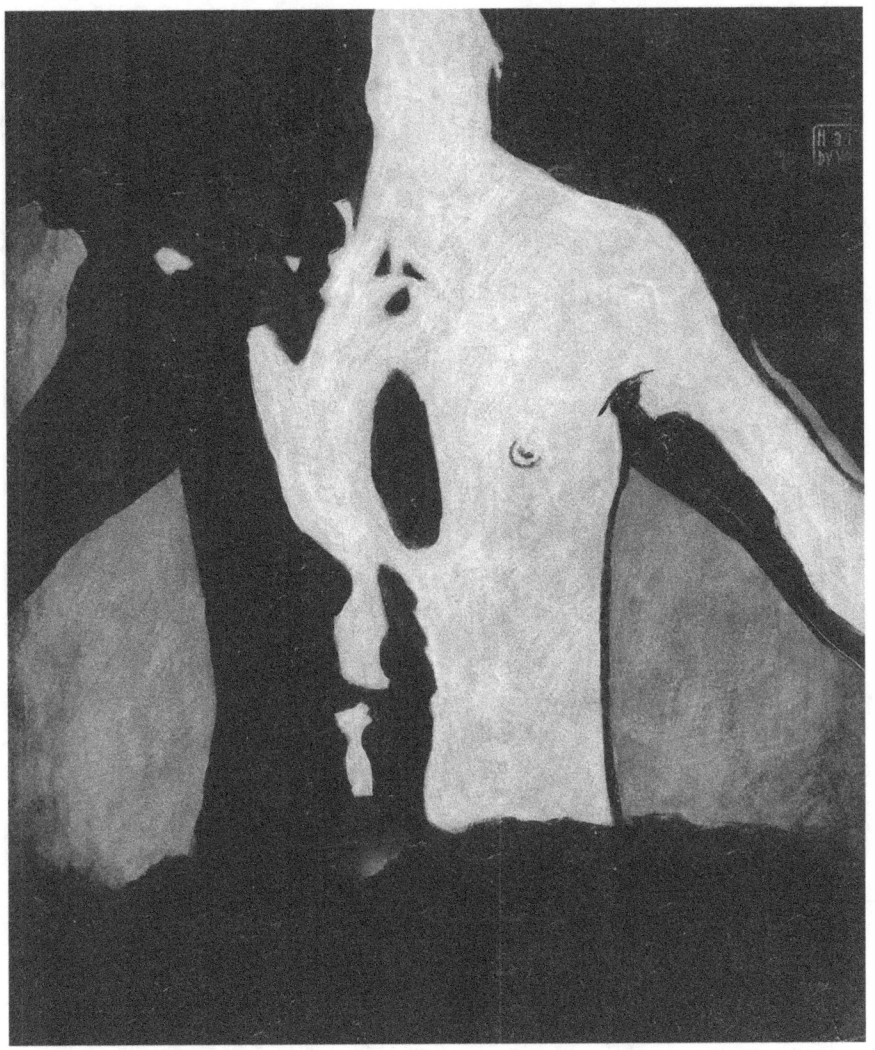

Acrylic painting

a moonlit desire
lunacy or fantasy
breathless wondering

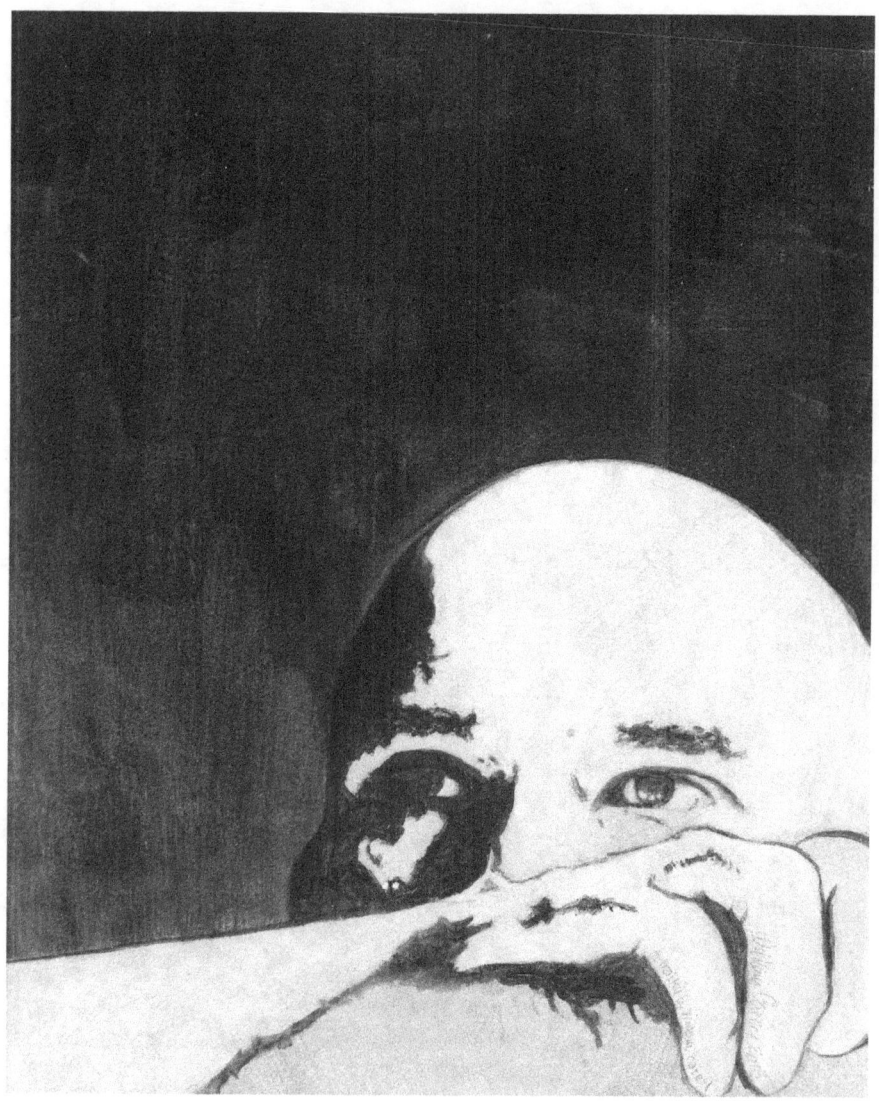

Acrylic painting

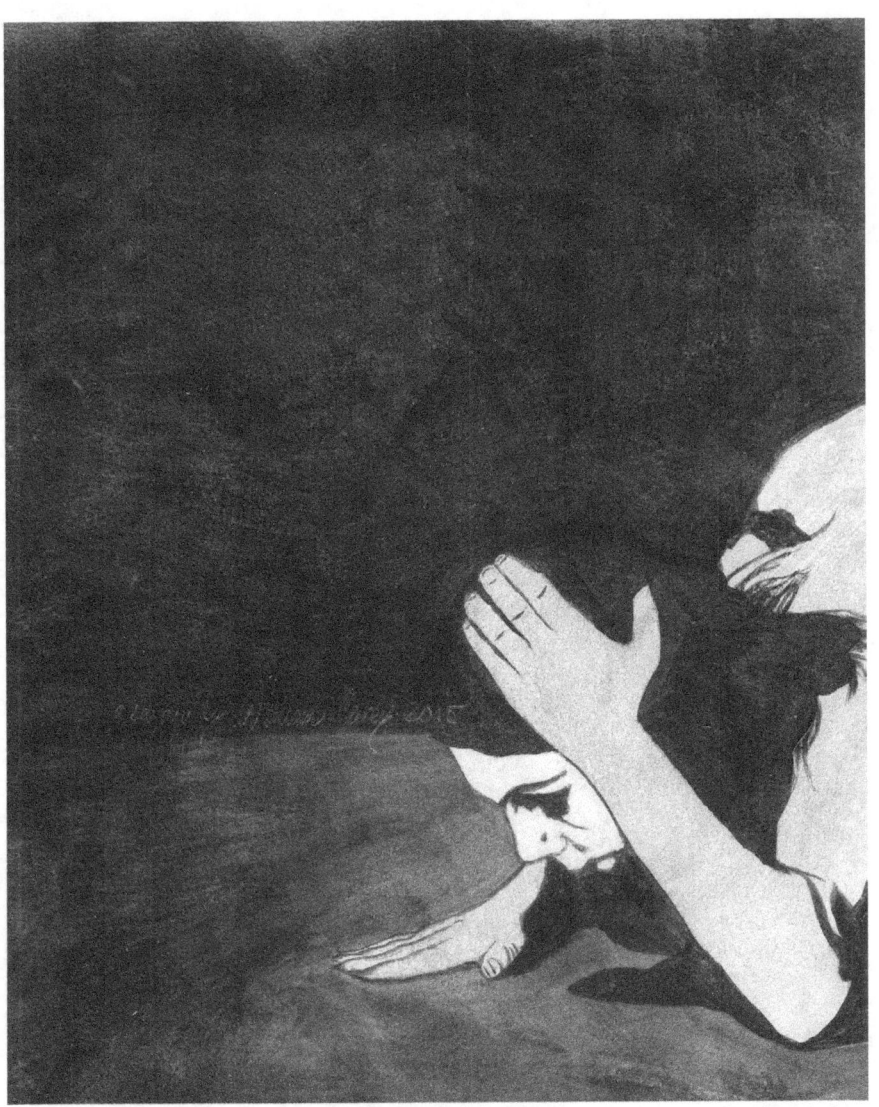

Acrylic painting

looking for her soul
zombie tries to remember
where she breathed her last

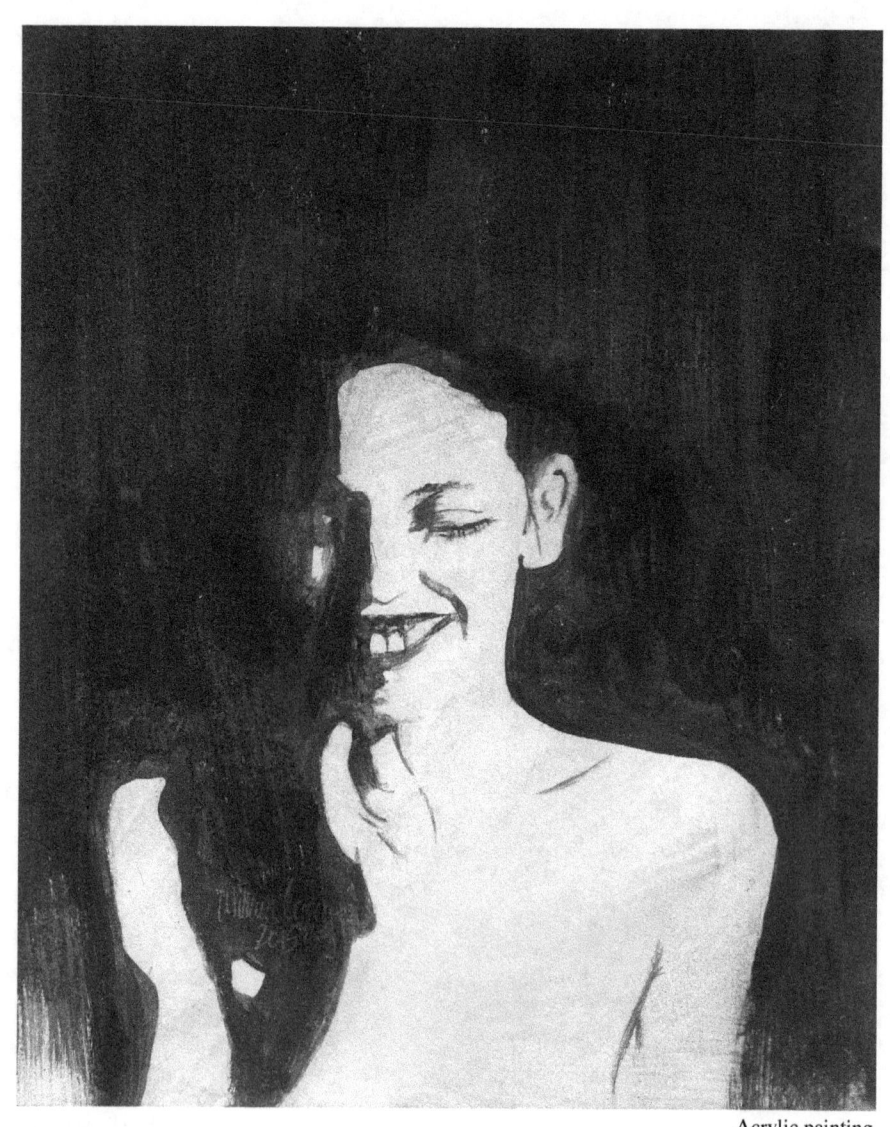

Acrylic painting

a private moment,
joyful giggle bubbles up,
tickling her chin

exposed outlier
pondering mysteries that
cannot be explained

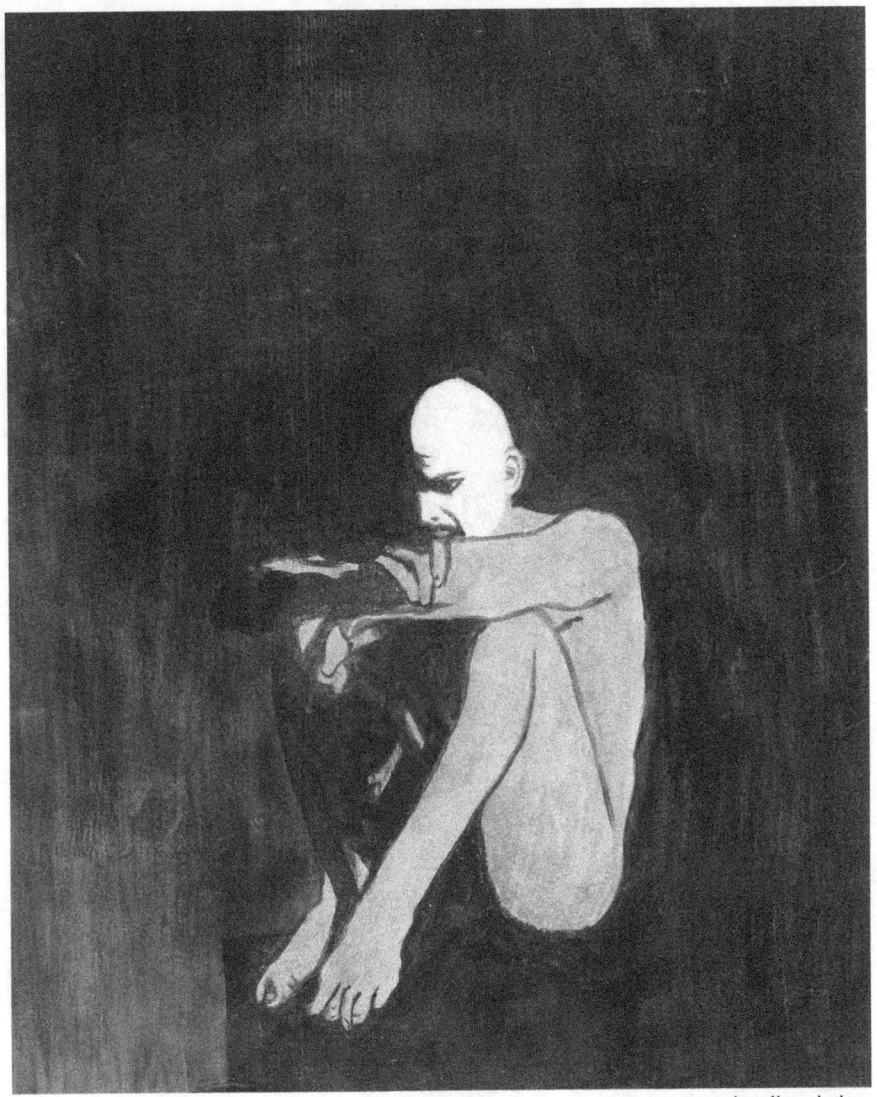

Acrylic painting

poet embracing
her emotions, awaiting
their inspiration

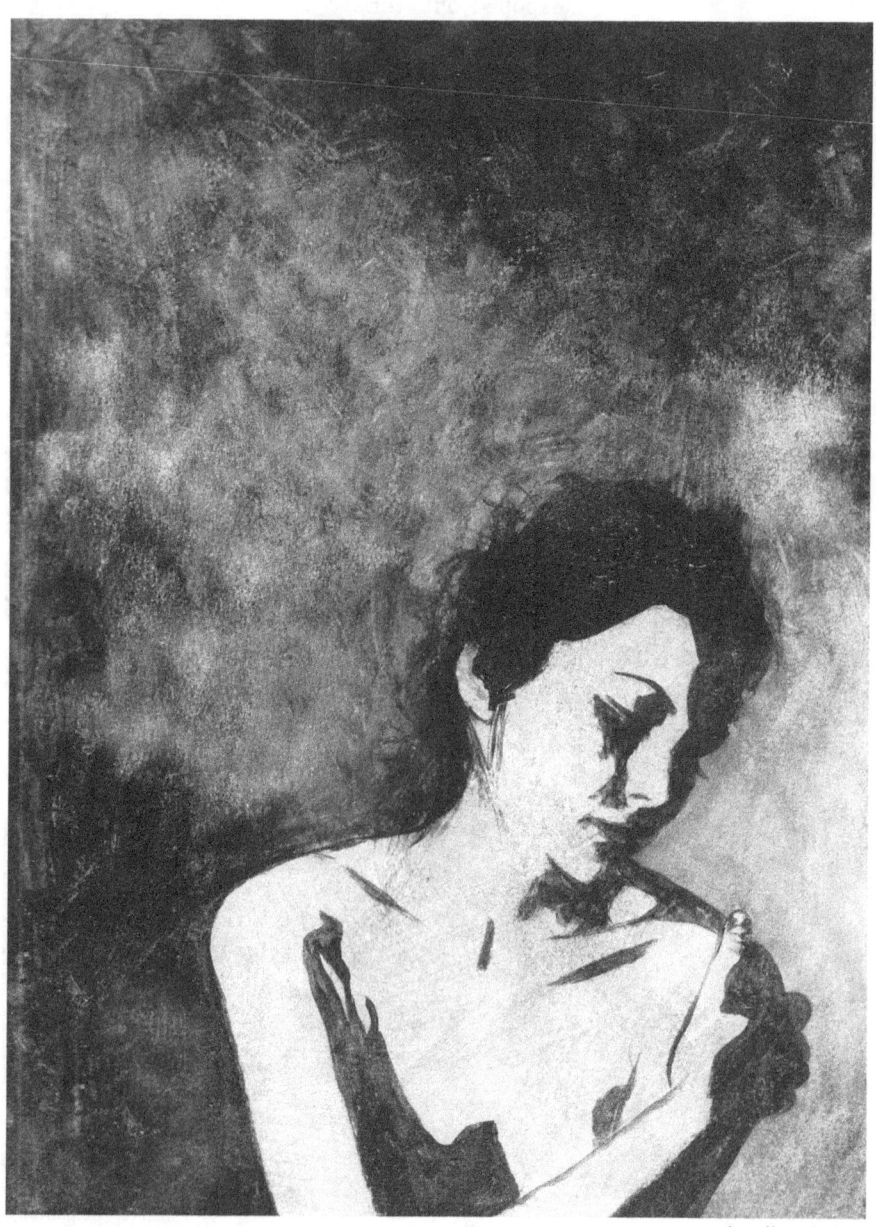

Acrylic painting

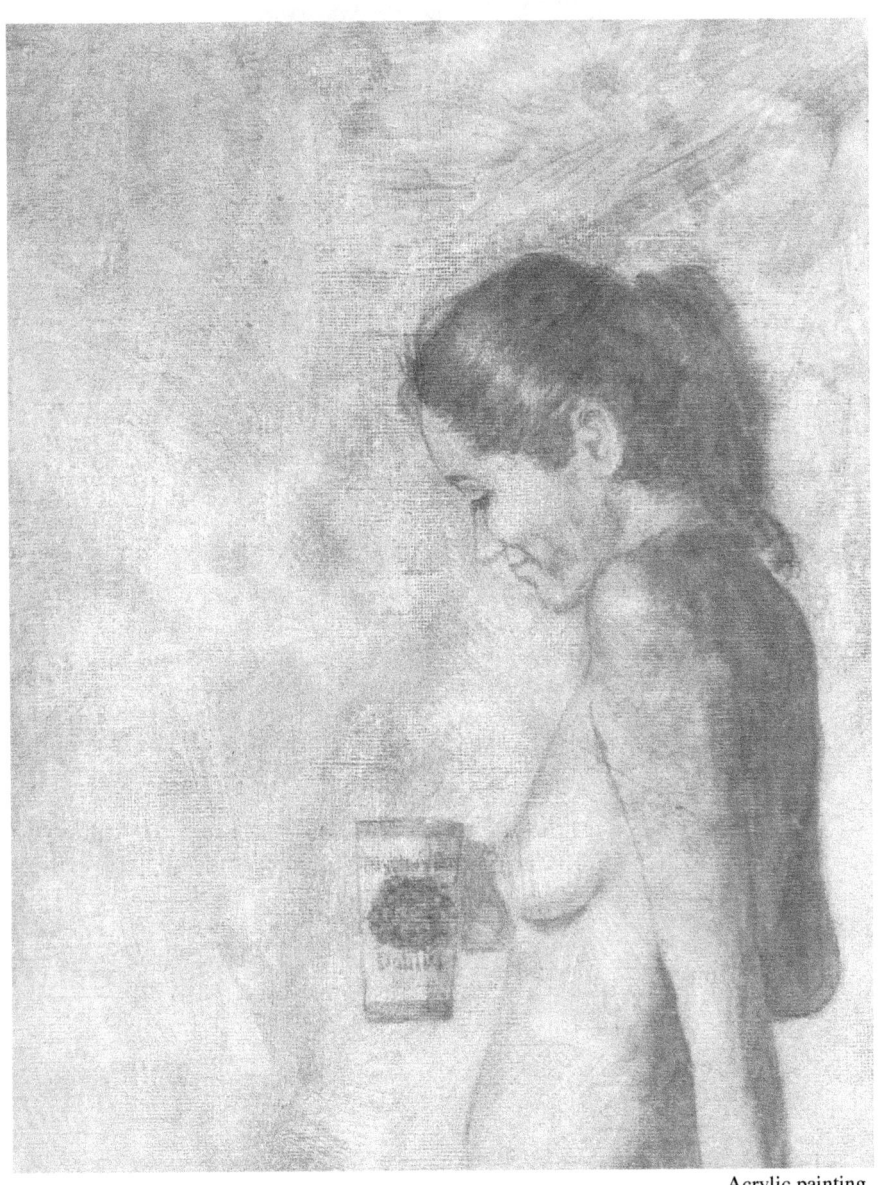

Acrylic painting

morning coffee muse
creating mysteries to
explain mysteries

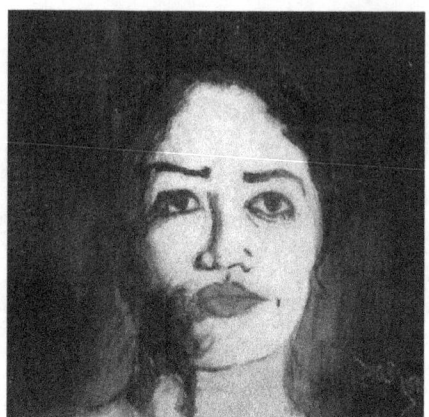

Acrylic painting

Haibun

Haibun is a combination of Haiku and prose that complement each other. In my case, sometimes the prose is written about the Haiku and in others the process is reversed. I find that all Haiku could become Haibun since they are a distillation of more complex observations or thoughts.

I many times ponder the deeper meaning of a Haiku but do not write those thoughts down. In the eight that follow, I have.

You will notice an ebb and flow of perceptions in the spiritual haibun. They were written at different periods of my own personal journey and reflect the attitudes that I held during those times.

```
I searched my old haunts
a ghost walking through a dream
a lost memory
```

When I first wrote this poem it was about an evening when I sought out a drinking establishment that I used to hang out in nine years before. It had been kind of a "Cheers" type place for me and I went back hoping that I might run into some of the people that I had known back in the day. I walked up to the bar and ordered a beer, looked around and realized that not only was there no one that I knew but no one over twenty-five. And being in my forties, I had become "a lost memory."

As time went on and my circumstances changed, my interpretation of the haiku changed. There was an existential period when I felt alone in a hostile environment; and was looking for a way out. This evolved.

Now I see it in a more Zen-like terms. With the "dream" being the illusion that is life and the haiku itself a koan to be solved.

---

koan: a paradoxical Zen riddle, used to provoke enlightenment

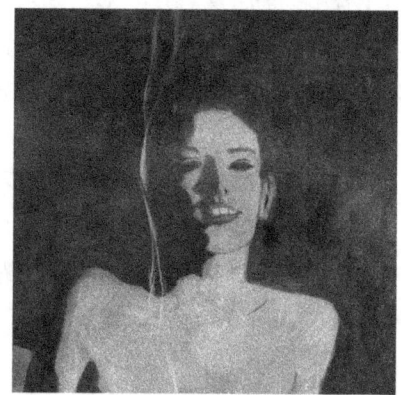

Acrylic painting

Everything we will
be doing tomorrow, we
will be doing now

*The only time we can do anything is **now**. We can plan for the future **now** and we can recall the past **now** but you cannot do anything in the future or the past. This is the eternal **now** of Zen Buddhism and it is not some profound mystical revelation, it is simply the way it is.*

*The whole eternal **now** concept brings up an interesting point about the past. Since the past can only be experienced **now**, it can only exist now. So it is not like some long road that we travel back on, but more like an invisible cloud of memories that surrounds us, mostly existing just below our consciousness that we become aware of when we remember something, **now**.*

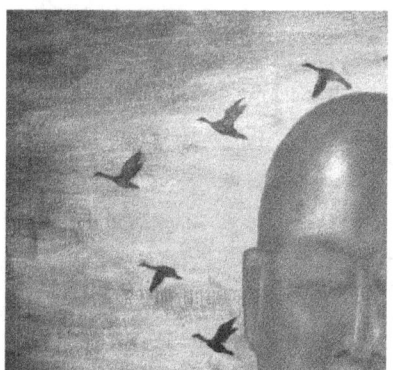
Acrylic painting

```
birds soar through sky
vibrating divinely
on subatomic wings
```

This was a reflection on the similarities between modern physics and eastern mysticism. Both in their own way, conclude that reality is an illusion.

By exploring the subatomic world with particle accelerators and mathematics, physicists have found that the smallest units of matter that they can discern are moving at incredible speeds. made up of energy and are surrounded by 99.9% empty space. So what we consider solid matter, in reality is not solid at all. It is an illusion.

Eastern mystics have intuitively maintained this premise. Reality is an all-inclusive vibrating manifestation and embodiment of a divine thought, not the separate solid mechanical construct that it appears to be.

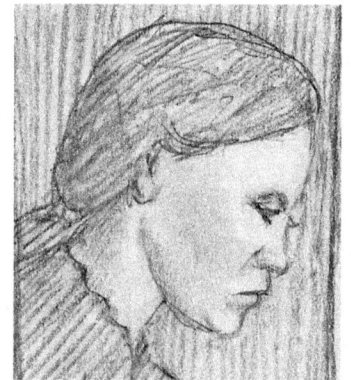

Graphite drawing

A seeker always...
for once I find... no longer
a seeker am I

Seekers of eternal truth all end up slamming into the wall of mystery: the holy mystery of Christianity, the void of the Tao Te Ching, the eternal now of Zen Buddhism. The greatest minds of the human race have wrestled with this. All have had to reach a compromise... faith.

Without faith there is eternal seeking. A vagabond soul; dissatisfied and full of yearning, bleeding energy. Faith is a tourniquet; it slows the bleeding and numbs the quest. It channels energy away from the impossible to the attainable. The abstract is captured in a definition where it can be looked at, studied, and put in your pocket.

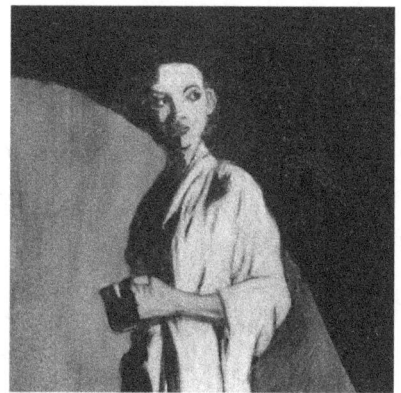
Acrylic painting

spry youthful spirit
facing an aging visage
reflecting mirror

Narcissis and Goldmund by Herman Hesse is a book that I have read at key times in my life: first in my 20's, then in my 40's and just recently in my 60's. Each time it was read from an altered perpective.

It is a story of Goldmund, a young boy, who is dropped off by his father to be raised in a monastery during the middle ages. As a young man he gets a taste of the pleasures and temptations of the outside world and deserts the monastery. He goes on to lead an adventurous and debauched life. Despite this, along the way he becomes an accomplished artist and sculptor. Later in the story he is rescued from certain death by his mentor, the monk Narcisses, and returns to the monastery. There he grows old producing a series of religious sculptures. Then as an old man, he gets restless and decides to to leave on one last adventure. At the beginning of his trek, he encounters a young girl and begins flirting with her with the intention of seducing her. But she sees him as a creepy old man and rebuffs him. He realizes that although he still feels young in his head, he has become an old man.

In my last reading of the book, I realized that every aging man has this revelation. One day he suddenly encounters an old man looking back at him in the mirror.

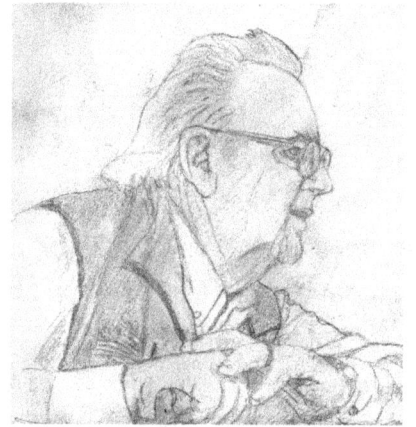

Graphite drawing

```
people's thoughts undressed
with a flash of emotion
naked minds exposed
```

A loud unruly child in a coffee shop gets a sharp look of disapproval from a customer engrossed in her laptop. Another lady gives the child's mother an understanding smile.

I am an avid people watcher. They have been the inspiration for many of the haiku and sketches that I have done over the years. I am fascinated by the amount of emotion that can be communicated through their body language or expressions alone.

As Shakespeare said, "all the world's a stage." For me it is also a studio, and all the players are models.

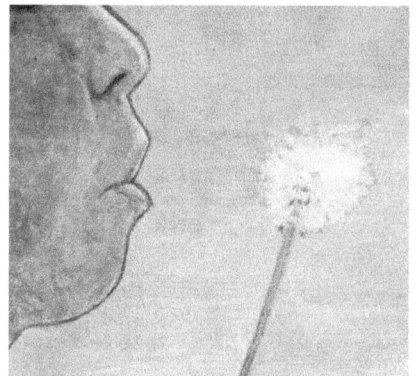

Acrylic painting

```
a yawn, a wisp of
clarity... sparkling thoughts
resolve into light
```

One sunny afternoon I was out in the back yard with my four-year old son. I was wearing a flowered shirt and a butterfly landed on my shoulder. My son noticed it and ran up and tried to catch it, It flew away and he chased after it. It eventually returned and once again lighted on my shoulder. Mike ran back and tried to catch it and again it flew off. It finally fluttered off out of the yard.

I have been meditating in one form or another for many years. This experience reminded me of how after a particularly exquisite meditation experience, I had tried to recreate it during my next meditation.

But of course, each experience is like the butterfly that landed on my shoulder that sunny afternoon. When I try to capture it, it flies away.

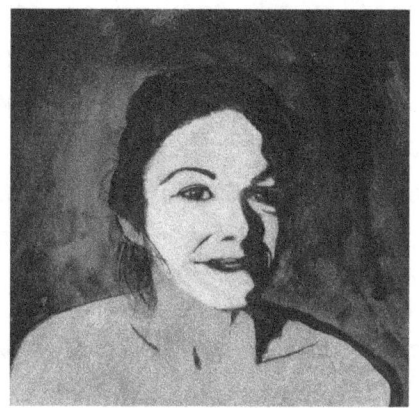

Acrylic painting

we are windows through
which God enjoys existence
for God's sake enjoy

When you bring a smile to a child's face the joy you have created reflects back, not only to you but through you to the source of creation. We are spiritual windows to and from the divine.

God created us to create our lives. Being that love and joy are the ideal state we all strive for, this must be the divine ideal also.

Based on this, I don't think that God enjoys or creates suffering. Only we can do that. We are given a choice. So for God's sake, enjoy.

About the author

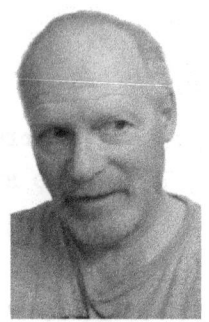

William Carey is an artist and Haiku Poet. He graduated from Illinois Wesleyan University with a BFA in Art. Since then he has made his living as a journeyman artist in the fine and graphic arts fields. He has found expression in painting, sculpture, graphic design. He has had showings of his work in Aurora, Geneva, and Chicago, IL.

Throughout his life he has been on an underlying spiritual quest. In an effort to make sense of these complex studies, he began to write Haiku, distilling them down to a simple 17 syllable essence. As time went on he began to write them on every subject.

If you have any comments or wish to purchase more copies of this book or prints, he can be contacted at wcareyartist@gmail.com.

Note: Traditional haiku has a seasonal element to it as many of the haiku in this book do. Those that do not contain that seasonal reference are considered a type of haiku called senryu and are mainly concerned with observations of human foibles.

www.ingramcontent.com/pod-product-compliance
Lightning Source LLC
Chambersburg PA
CBHW071615170526
45166CB00003B/1087